THE WATSON GORDON
LECTURE 2009

THE WATSON GORDON
LECTURE 2009

The Renaissance Image Unveiled:
From Madonna to Venus

PAUL HILLS

NATIONAL GALLERIES OF SCOTLAND

in association with
THE UNIVERSITY OF EDINBURGH
and
VARIE

*

Published by the Trustees
of the National Galleries of Scotland, Edinburgh
in association with The University of Edinburgh and VARIE
© The author and the Trustees of the National Galleries of Scotland 2010
ISBN 978 1 906270 34 6
Frontispiece: detail from Titian *Diana and Actaeon* (fig.18)
Designed and typeset in Adobe Arno by Dalrymple
Printed and bound on Hello Matt 150gsm
by OZGraf SA, Poland

FOREWORD

The publication of this series of lectures has roots deep in the cultural history of Scotland's capital. The Watson Gordon Chair of Fine Art at the University of Edinburgh was approved in October 1872, when the University Court accepted the offer of Mr Henry Watson C.A. and his sister Frances to endow a chair in memory of their brother Sir John Watson Gordon (1788–1864). Sir John, Edinburgh's most successful portrait painter in the decades following Sir Henry Raeburn's death in 1823, had a European reputation, and had also been President of the Royal Scottish Academy. Funds became available on Henry Watson's death in 1879, and the first incumbent, Gerard Baldwin Brown, took up his post the following year. Thus, as one of his successors, Giles Robertson explained in his inaugural lecture of 1972, the Watson Gordon Professorship can 'fairly claim to be the senior full-time chair in the field of Fine Art in Britain'.

The annual Watson Gordon Lecture was established in 2006, following the 125th anniversary of the Chair. We are most grateful for the generous and enlightened support of Robert Robertson and the R.& S.B. Clark Charitable Trust (E.C. Robertson Fund) for this series which demonstrates the fruitful collaboration between the University of Edinburgh and the National Galleries of Scotland.

The fourth Watson Gordon Lecture was given by Paul Hills of the Courtauld Institute of Art, London, on 12 November 2009. Professor Hills has published widely on Italian Renaissance art, exploring important themes, such as light and colour, from original angles. In his enthralling lecture he explains how veils – by masking and revealing – could suggest associations of birth, death and rebirth. Through subtle analysis of works of art his lecture illuminates the delicate process of interpreting Renaissance paintings and their elusive meanings.

RICHARD THOMSON
Watson Gordon Professor of Fine Art,
University of Edinburgh

JOHN LEIGHTON
Director-General,
National Galleries of Scotland

ACKNOWLEDGEMENTS

I should like to thank Professor Richard Thomson for his kind invitation to give the 2009 Watson Gordon Lecture. I much appreciated his enthusiasm for my subject, his constant support, and wonderful hospitality. The experience of getting to know the paintings in Edinburgh proved to be extraordinarily pleasurable and illuminating. When I made a research trip to Edinburgh in August 2009, the staff of the National Galleries of Scotland were generous with their help and advice. I would particularly like to thank Aidan Weston-Lewis of the Curatorial Department, Patricia Allerston in Education, the librarian Kerry Eldon in the National Gallery Archive & Library, and Olivia Sheppard in the Publishing Department. Roger Tarr, who knows the Italian paintings in Edinburgh so well, made several incisive comments after my lecture. Over several years of thinking about curtains and drapery in Renaissance art many friends and colleagues have given me references, shared ideas and criticised my flights of fancy. I extend my thanks to Irene Brook, Joanna Cannon, Michael Douglas Scott, John Dury, Antony Eastmond, Caroline Elam, John Lowden and Peter Stewart.

THE RENAISSANCE
IMAGE UNVEILED: FROM MADONNA
TO VENUS

When we visit an Italian church today, it is only on rare occasions that we witness the shutters of a tabernacle being opened, or a curtain in front of an altarpiece being raised, or a smaller devotional panel being unveiled. Nor, when we visit a gallery or palace, are we likely to see a curtain or drape being lifted to uncover a painting of an erotic nature.[1] Accustomed to the experience of paintings as continually on show, it is difficult to appreciate how the alternation between unveiling and covering images relates to their narrative content and physical structure. Between the late thirteenth century and the sixteenth – from the era of Duccio to that of Raphael and Titian – the veils and curtains that traditionally indicated sacred presence and its revelation were transformed into instruments of artistic epiphany. One form of veiling was not simply replaced by another, but rather the cult function of veiling became absorbed within the demonstration of art. Of course this is a vast theme, but when I was invited to deliver the Watson Gordon lecture, I quickly realised that the National Gallery of Scotland is home to a number of paintings that illuminate this topic in compelling ways. Drawing largely, but not exclusively, on paintings in Edinburgh, I hope that what follows may open up one path through the labyrinth of Renaissance veils.

The revelation of sacred images was most emphatic in the physical form of tabernacles, and nowhere more so than in the monumental tabernacle in Orsanmichele in Florence, designed by Andrea Orcagna in the 1350s to house the panel of the *Madonna and Child with Angels* by Bernardo Daddi (fig.1). It is a freestanding structure, domed just as the cathedral of Florence dedicated to Santa Maria del Fiore was intended to be.[2] Brocaded curtains, carved in stone, and elaborately gathered and gilded, frame Bernardo Daddi's panel. They honour the Virgin and demarcate an inner sanctuary within the architectural structure. Statutes of 1294 and 1333, relating to an earlier painting on the same site, stipulated that the image of Our Lady was to be kept covered by a veil (*velo*) – 'or indeed with subtle

FIG.1 | ANDREA ORCAGNA (*c*.1308–1368)
Tabernacle in Orsanmichele, Florence (view from front with Bernardo Daddi's *Madonna and Child with Angels* visible through arch), *c*.1359

and refined veils of silk' – and that the image should only be uncovered on Sundays and feast days with two torches lit.[3] Yet the rules of viewing and reverencing the image were not quite absolute in the face of worldly authority: if distinguished foreigners visited on other days the Madonna could be uncovered under a special licence, if only for a short time. The open arcades at the front and sides that frame a space in front of the Madonna in Orcagna's tabernacle have intricately carved valances within the arches; beneath them grooves within the stonework indicate that shutters were originally installed to close these arches.[4] These valances and shutters heightened the sense of passage between real and fictive worlds.

The opening and closing enacted on a monumental scale in Orsanmichele was more modestly replicated in many smaller folding triptychs, such as the one attributed to Bernardo Daddi in Edinburgh.[5] Here, unusually, an enthroned Madonna occupies the inside of the right wing rather than the centre (fig.2). As Mother and Child gaze at each other, Christ lifts one hand to the Virgin's face and with the other grasps the edge of the veil that hangs down across her chest. The motif of the Child holding onto the Virgin's veil is one that was repeated in many panels painted by Bernardo Daddi and his workshop. In the Edinburgh triptych the veil is so diaphanous that it would be barely visible but for Christ's gesture.

This intimate motif of Christ reaching towards his Mother or her veil has its origin in the type of Byzantine icon known as the *Kykkotissa*, which was transformed around 1300 by the Sienese master Duccio.[6] What Duccio and his followers discovered in the play of gestures and veils was made possible – and plausible – by developments in the technology of silk weaving. I want to consider this for a moment. It is the story of how a change in material production brought about a striking inversion of a key theological symbol.

By tradition and according to etymology a veil was an opaque cloth that completely obscured or hid from view whatever lay beneath or behind it. This was the essential meaning of the veil or *velum* in the Old Testament. Such a cloth that hides from view was what was intended by God's instructions to Moses to 'make a veil of blue and purple and scarlet stuff and fine twined linen', and to bring the Ark of the Covenant within this veil, which would separate 'the holy place from the most holy'.[7] The only mortal permitted to pass through this obscuring veil into

FIG.2 | BERNARDO DADDI
(ACTIVE *c*.1300–DIED 1348)
Madonna and Child with Angels
(detail of right wing of triptych), 1338
Tempera, silver (tarnished) and gold on panel
Wing (right): 57.7 × 15.2cm
National Gallery of Scotland, Edinburgh

the Holy of Holies was the High Priest bearing a sacrificial offering. Once the Ark received its fixed abode within the temple in Jerusalem, this veil became the veil of the temple – the same veil that, according to Mark's gospel, was rent in two from top to bottom at the moment that Christ died on the Cross.[8] St Paul argued, in what was to become a celebrated passage in his Epistle to the Hebrews, that thanks to Christ's death on the Cross, the High Priest entering the Holy of Holies was replaced by Christ, who was himself both priest and sacrifice. The veil that prevented mortals from seeing salvation had been done away – torn apart – by the sacrifice of Christ. Using memorably strange imagery, Paul declared in Hebrews that 'Christ's flesh is the veil', and in Corinthians that the 'veil is done away in Christ'.[9] In other words, what had previously been hidden from the Jews was now revealed to all believers.

With the development in the Middle Ages of the technology of weaving, it became possible to produce gauzy fabrics that allowed what lay beneath to be seen through them. By the late thirteenth century, when silk manufacture was expanding rapidly in Tuscan cities, semi-transparent veils could both preserve a token of modesty while at the same time enhancing feminine beauty and allure. The social distinction offered by fine textiles proved irresistible to the mercantile elites who could afford them. In painted images Duccio led the way by showing how diaphanous veils might honour the most gracious Virgin Mary. Soon abandoning the tight-fitting cap or *ciuffa* worn by Byzantine Madonnas, he clothed the Virgin in lighter, looser veils. In the *Madonna and Child* in the National Gallery of Umbria, Perugia, six angels, resting on the raised moulding of the frame, gaze down in adoration (fig.3).[10] The angels' hands are cupped over the raised arch in casual, rapt gestures of adoration and wonder. What they cue the beholder to gaze upon is in part concealed: the Christ Child's lower body is covered by a cloth of royal purple – a gorgeous complement to the gold – whereas his upper body is draped in a gauzy cloth through which his mortal flesh can be seen. He clasps this veil at his shoulder, while with the same hand he also gathers up his Mother's more opaque white veil. Like a jewelled fibula or brooch fastening an antique cloak or *chlamys*, Christ's hand unites the veil that is his flesh with the veil of his Mother who gave him birth.[11] Thanks to the technology of weaving semi-transparent fabrics, Christ's flesh can now be seen through the veil. Far from being simply an illustration of the theological trope of veil and flesh, Duccio's painting realises and extends it in a manner that Paul could never have anticipated. It is a perfect example of what Jeffrey Hamburger has described as the creative contribution of medieval art to theology: as images became central to devotional practices so 'presence replaced absence, visibility superseded invisibility'.[12] The diaphanous veil has become the sign of seeing salvation.

It was one of the creative contributions of figurative art to introduce play between the Madonna's protective mantle and her veil or headdress.[13] The mantle or cloak became a highly adaptable image of the communion of believers gathered within the shelter of the Christian *ecclesia*. In the later Middle Ages artists were called upon to produce countless images of the Madonna and Child: trying out variations in the draping of the two figures and how they interacted, they hit upon new ways of presenting or disclosing the relation of Mother and Son. It was the search for variation within a frequently repeated subject, rather than theological sophistication, that generated fresh nuances. Some artists repeated formulae unthinkingly, whereas other artists uncovered new significance in the tender human image at the centre of Christian devotion. Even if a transparent veil – sign of Christ's Eucharistic flesh – was not always described, the particular draping, encircling and knotting of mantles, sashes and girdles afforded outward and visible signs of the bond between Virgin and Child. Consider, for example, Lorenzo Monaco's panel of the Madonna in Edinburgh (fig.4).[14]

Quite deliberately, Lorenzo allows the lion-headed faldstool and its golden cloth to blend with the *campo d'oro* or field of gold, thereby ensuring that the pliant draperies of the Madonna and Child hold the stage. Christ, now an older child dressed in princely robe, stands upon his Mother's lap. She steadies him with her left hand, partially enfolding him in her dark blue mantle. What is presented here, within the enveloping mantle, is a movement from containment to disclosure. Both the Mother and the Child address the beholder with their gaze, and their gestures are ostensive: with one hand Christ holds the scroll and with the other he draws his Mother's blue veil towards him. Quite deliberately, Lorenzo has arranged the extremity of the Madonna's veil to hang in folds at the centre of

[13]

FIG.3 | DUCCIO (ACTIVE 1278–1318)
Madonna and Child with Six Angels, 1300–5
Tempera on wood 97 × 63cm
National Gallery of Umbria, Perugia

FIG.4 | LORENZO MONACO AND WORKSHOP (BEFORE 1375–*c.*1425)
*Madonna and Child Enthroned, c.*1418
Tempera and gold on panel 101.6 × 61.7cm
National Gallery of Scotland, Edinburgh

the panel, and with equal deliberation he has dressed Christ in a girdle of precisely the same pale blue, and knotted it just below the Child's slightly feminised chest in order to replicate the Madonna's veil. Thanks to this rhyming of colour and folds the symbolic bond between Madonna and Child is made visible.

I have dwelt upon this modest painting as it may serve to introduce an aspect of fifteenth-century images of the Madonna that has been largely overlooked by scholars. It concerns the Madonna's girdle, and how that girdle may be bound up with imagery of swaddling, clothing and unveiling Christ.

In a *Madonna and Child*, now in the Louvre (fig.5), painted by the Florentine Alessio Baldovinetti around 1464, swaddling and veil are presented in significant conjunction. The infant Christ, clothed in only a belt of swaddling just above his waist, holds up its loose end towards his Mother. This strip of cloth passes in front of his navel and up towards the Virgin's womb, almost as if it was a material token of the umbilical cord which once united them.[15] Baldovinetti echoed the winding shape of this swaddling in the meander of the river in the distant valley, thereby extending this intimate sign into the larger world of creation. But the swaddling is not the only significant cloth in this picture: a translucent veil, just like the one the Madonna wears over her hair, lies over the marble ledge, extending from just in front of the Child's feet and up over the scarlet cushion. It is bordered with two threads of white, and like the Madonna's veil it is painted with tiny dots and fringed with bolder dots in Baldovinetti's characteristic technique, which – as Caroline Elam pointed out in an earlier Watson Gordon lecture – E.M. Forster gently mocked as 'painting dottily'.[16] As an artist still using egg tempera to bind his pigments, Baldovinetti deployed fine dots rather than oil glazes to describe a diaphanous fabric. In the *Madonna and Child* in the Louvre, Christ leans back with one arm resting on the cushion, crumpling the veil with the impress of his palm. Towering above him, his Mother has joined her hands in devotion, as if to acknowledge her Son's meaningful gestures of offering her the swaddling band and touching the translucent veil beneath him. Together, the Child's gesture of unwinding the cloth and impressing his hand upon the translucent veil may be read as alluding to the display of the Eucharistic Body of Christ.

The relic of the Madonna's girdle or *cintola*, preserved in a shrine in the

FIG.5 | ALESSIO BALDOVINETTI (*c*.1425–1499)
*Madonna and Child, c.*1464
Tempera on panel 106 × 75cm
Musée du Louvre, Paris

cathedral at Prato, not far from Florence, was celebrated for its powers in assisting successful conception and childbirth.[17] In the Renaissance the fertility of a bride was of prime concern, and decorative belts were often given to the bride at her betrothal.[18] Then as now, an expectant mother was referred to in Italian as 'incinta'. Significantly, swaddling bands were almost interchangeable with girdles; both were used as charms in pregnancy and childbirth. As Jacqueline Musacchio has remarked 'illuminated scrolls based on the length of the body of Christ and inscribed with prayers to the Virgin and Saint Margaret, were used as girdles for pregnant women, and were actually wound around their bodies during labour'.[19]

With this in mind we may notice how some fifteenth-century painters allude – albeit in understated fashion – to the kinship between the Madonna's girdle and the Christ Child's swaddling. Several panels by Carlo Crivelli, a painter active in the Marches (eastern central Italy) in the second half of the fifteenth century, hint at this affinity. In the central panel of Crivelli's altarpiece for the cathedral in Ascoli, for example, Christ is only swaddled around his chest at a height matching that of the sash-like girdle or *cintola* knotted beneath his Mother's bust.[20] Although girdle and swaddling are evidently separate cloths, they are matched in their type of plain linen fabric and in their whiteness – a whiteness that in turn links them to the pallor of the Virgin's headdress. Typically, Crivelli has taken pains to delineate the fine tassels that hang from the ends of this headdress and from the loose ends of the swaddling.

Crivelli's attention to every tassel, crease and fold borders on the fetishistic, but we should note – as Ronald Lightbown has done – that his cloths are charged with meaning. In the centre of his great altarpiece from San Domenico in Ascoli, now in the National Gallery in London (fig.6), the Child is slumped forward with his chin resting on his Mother's hand.[21] He is dressed in a white tunic or vest. Over this tunic, falling in folds upon his Mother's lap, is a diaphanous veil which the Madonna holds up between her finger and thumb in a symbolic gesture of revelation. The raised triangle of veil appears as a miniature tent or tabernacle, and once again the transparency of the veil – so finely rendered by Crivelli's brush – functions as a sign that the *velum* that once hid the Holy of Holies has been torn apart so that now the faithful can see salvation.

[18]

FIG.6 | CARLO CRIVELLI (*c*.1430/5–*c*.1494)
Madonna and Child, from
The Demidoff Altarpiece, 1476
Tempera on lime 148.6 × 63.5cm
The National Gallery, London

FIG.7 | FERRARESE SCHOOL
Madonna and Child with Two Angels,
late 15th century
Tempera, oil and gold on panel 58.5 × 44cm
National Gallery of Scotland, Edinburgh

I hope this discussion of girdle, swaddling bands and veil may open up new ways to think about one of the most fascinating pictures in Edinburgh, the little panel of the Madonna and Child attributed to a Ferrarese Master (fig.7). I am not directly concerned here with the tricky question of attribution, but I agree with the scholarly consensus that locates it in the orbit of Ferrara.[22] Some critics date it to the 1470s, though it could plausibly belong to the late 1460s, when the art of Piero della Francesca – who had painted in Ferrara early in his career – was still a vital influence.[23] This would place the Edinburgh Madonna somewhere between Baldovinetti's of about 1464 and Crivelli's Madonnas, which date from the mid 1470s.[24] Both the Ferrarese master and Crivelli frame the Virgin's head in a white headdress with corners lifted by the wind, probably because both artists share roots in Paduan art at mid-century where this kind of animation of drapery was common.

Less concerned than Crivelli with the materiality of textiles, the Ferrarese master activates the symbolic field more evocatively. The veil of the temple rent in two at the Crucifixion is here transposed into a parchment or skin on its stretcher, which has been ripped open to reveal the Madonna and Child and two adoring angels.[25] On the Ferrarese panel, as one physical skin is torn away, the beholder is reminded that the sacred image is no more than another membrane or veil on which corporeal forms are figured only as a means of apprehending spiritual or incorporeal truths. White clouds drift across a pale blue sky and distant hills are veiled in mist.[26] These intangible distances are set against the hard, tactile presence of the frame. At the bottom left, within the imperfect sinful world of the spectator, a fly has landed on the torn membrane. Our Ferrarese painter delights in twisted drapes, in flaps and folds. He has shaped the Madonna's headdress in undulations and lifted its corners hanging below her shoulders, gently taking up the rhythm of the curling edges of the ripped membrane. Unlike Crivelli's headdresses, it is plain, abstracted, without fastenings or tassels or patterned borders. Its candid whiteness contrasts with the drab buff of the torn backing. It seems to be held open around the Virgin's face and shoulders by an unseen breath or *pneuma*. Together, the torn membrane and the open veil act in concert, figuring disclosure.

The Madonna greets the beholder with a raised hand and open palm. She sees and listens, her headdress arching back in a generous cup around her left ear. In her right hand, resting on her knee, she holds a pomegranate, fruit of many seeds, familiar symbol of fertility and resurrection or rebirth. On the other knee, paired with the pomegranate, the Child lolls forward in sleep, and steadies himself by hanging onto the pendant sash of his Mother's girdle. He is totally naked. The meaning of this configuration is not predetermined; it is not constructed from a set of symbols, it is generated in the play between them, a play that the painter discovers. Pomegranate and girdle may both signify fertility. Christ sleeping, naked except for coral bracelets and necklace, may allude to his death and Passion. Christ's grasp of his Mother's girdle may be a reminder of their physical bond. But these potential meanings are only realised and apprehended within the larger pictorial field of contrasts of weight and weightlessness – the heaviness of the Child leaning forward compared to the tripping lightness of the scarlet-slippered angels, for instance, or the aerial gleam of the clouds and of the Madonna's billowing veil compared to the massive arches of the bridge on which she sits and to the sepulchral depths beneath it.

Contrasts of scale render the image mysterious. The torn backing and wooden stretcher are close, within touch of the beholder. The rocky edge that butts up against the fictive frame belongs to a different order, a larger scale, whereas the hem of the Virgin's robe, lying in folds upon the bare ground, returns us to an intimate measure. She sits upon a bridge of classic simplicity and weight worthy of Leon Battista Alberti – who had been resident in Ferrara at the court of Leonello d'Este in the 1440s, and who had demonstrated the Roman sense of *gravitas* in his architecture in the Tempio Malatestiana at Rimini. This bridge lends the Madonna a monumental presence as she towers over her diminutive Child.

These contrasts of scale, and shifts in the register of illusion, have reminded critics of devices in the most inventive book illuminations around 1470, such as the frontispiece to the *Decretum* of canon and civil law by Gratian, which was printed in Venice by Nicholas Jenson and illuminated by Girolamo da Cremona (fig.8).[27] A luxury incunabulum emulating a fine illuminated manuscript, it is printed on parchment, and – as if to draw attention to this conspicuous expense – Girolamo's frontispiece plays with the visual conceit of a torn sheet of parchment. Its edges curl forward, catching the light and casting shadows in a manner that is strongly reminiscent of the ripped membrane of the Ferrarese Madonna.

Now although these parallels are striking, what is without precedent in book illumination is the prominence given in our picture to the fictive wooden stretcher. Pictorially it is an emphatic presence, unmistakably of wood. It furnishes a solid frame that emphasises the perspicuity of the aperture. In that sense it may recall Alberti's image of painting as equivalent to a view through an open window.[28] It is worth remembering at this point that casements in fifteenth-century Italy were rarely glazed; instead they were sealed with waxed paper or cloth. A hinged casement with a membrane of paper or cloth is represented in some fifteenth-century paintings.[29] Could it be that what is described here is the torn paper or cloth of a window casement? Or could it even be a sly reference to Alberti's *'velum'* or 'veil loosely woven of fine thread' which he invented as an aid to rendering the correct intersection of the visual pyramid?[30]

The problem with such readings is that they have little symbolic and devotional resonance. Rather than appealing to Alberti, we should dwell upon the emphatic presence of wood and of the nails that penetrate the parchment or skin and enter the wood. To a devout viewer this would recall the nails that passed through Christ's skin and entered the wood of the Cross. One or two of the nails have been pulled out and made visible – notably at the bottom left corner. Although there are many more nails than the three that were used in the Crucifixion, an allusion to the Passion and wounding of Christ accords with the solemn mood of the painting.

In her *Dialogue of the Seraphic Virgin*, St Catherine of Siena used an image – extended over several chapters – of the 'Bridge' of Christ.[31] The sin of Adam, she writes, had opened a deep gulf between earth and heaven, which was filled with the turbulent waters of mortal life, waters so dangerous that no soul might pass over them without drowning in sin. Christ crucified is the bridge or way of salvation thrown over these waters. Although in the Ferrarese painting 'turbulent waters' are not conspicuous, it is noticeable that in the distance there is a second bridge crossing a wider expanse of water. The sleeping Child, the rent membrane, the sharp nails, the two bridges, all suggest death and rites of passage. As in the

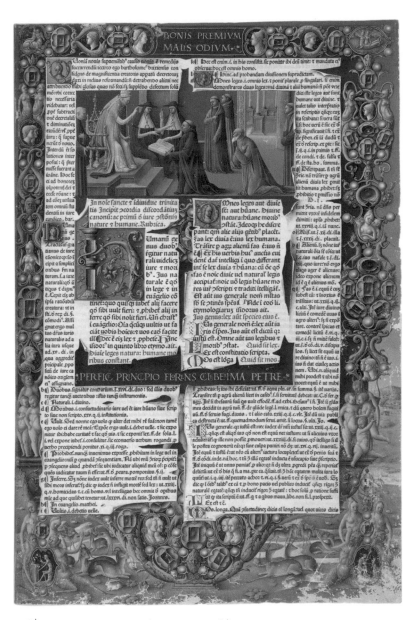

FIG.8 | GIROLAMO DA CREMONA (ACTIVE 1451–1483)
Gratian presents the Pope with his Concordance of Canon Law, frontispiece to
the *Decretum* of Gratian, printed in Venice by Nicholas Jenson in 1477
Forschungsbibliothek, Gotha, Mon. Typ.1477, 2 (12), folio 2r

FIG.9 | FILIPPINO LIPPI (c.1457–1504)
The Nativity with Two Angels, possibly early 1490s
Tempera, oil and gold on panel 25 × 37cm
National Gallery of Scotland, Edinburgh

other fifteenth-century paintings of the Madonna and Child I have discussed, imagery of girdles, veils and membranes address the fundamental themes of birth, death and rebirth.

Although these paintings may be illuminated by iconographic inquiry, what is remarkable is how they give symbolic form to a life experience that has come to be called 'abjection'. As formulated by Julia Kristeva, abjection describes both the traumatic separation of the child from an undifferentiated relationship with its mother as well as the expulsion of bodily fluids.[32] It is this experience that establishes the sense of bodily boundaries, the distinction of inner and outer, of the ego

FIG.10 | FILIPPINO LIPPI (c.1457–1504)
Pietà (The Dead Christ Mourned by Nicodemus and Two Angels), c.1500
Oil (and possibly tempera) on panel 17.5 × 33.3cm
Samuel H. Kress Collection
National Gallery of Art, Washington DC

and the non-ego. Now it is striking that the cult of the Virgin, which developed so strongly from the twelfth century onwards, insisted on her attachment to her Son – as his Mother and his Bride – and their painful separation. The pattern of joy alternating with sorrow, of being united, parted and reunited, runs through the Gospel narrative and is elaborated with great feeling and pathos in the pictorial tradition of the late Middle Ages. In psychoanalytic terms it is as if the separation of mother and child is reiterated, extended, never quite completed. The trauma of birth is repeated in the death and Passion of Christ, when the Virgin, standing at the foot of the Cross, swoons and suffers birth-pangs in her compassion or co-passion for her Son.[33] Significantly, the boundaries of Christ's body on the Cross are pierced by the nails and the lance; and from the wound in his side blood and water issue forth. Bodily fluids are very much part of this myth. As Caroline Bynum has shown, the Passion narrative can almost be read as an inversion of the Nativity in which the roles of the Virgin and her Son are matched: 'medieval writers spoke of Jesus as a mother who lactates and gives birth. They saw the flesh of God as clothing taken from Mary's flesh … The wound of Christ and the breast of Mary are clearly parallel …'.[34] Medieval texts and images dwelt on the closeness and the separation between Mother and Son, envisaging scenes never described in the Bible, such as Christ taking Leave of his Mother and the Virgin's Lamentation over his body after it had been taken down from the Cross. The hymn *Stabat Mater*, sometimes attributed to the Franciscan poet Jacopone da Todi, expresses the sorrow of the Mother standing beneath the Cross, at once close to her Son and cut off from him. In paintings of the Dormition of the Virgin they are shown reunited, with the Risen Christ holding the child-like figure of the Virgin's soul wrapped in a chrysalis of white cloth or swaddling. In all these scenes of Nativity, Passion, Dormition and Resurrection, veils, girdles, swaddling, cerements and shrouds are key accessories. They bind and loose; they indicate intimate connection or rupture; they figure openness to the world or closure and secrecy.

Filippino Lippi, like his father Filippo, was a virtuoso in describing diaphanous veils that bind and loose. In his paintings of the Nativity he emphasised the sacrificial and Eucharistic nature of the body of Christ. The National Gallery of Scotland's small painting of *The Nativity with Two Angels* (fig.9) is similar in composition and significance to the predella of *The Dead Christ Mourned by Nicodemus and Two Angels* in the National Gallery of Art in Washington (fig.10).[35] The setting in both is sepulchral. The Nativity cave-cum-stable is transformed into a rustic tabernacle, a shrine. In the Nativity, the two angels lift and open the Virgin's blue mantle in a manner that recalls the type known as the Madonna of Mercy, but here it is an act of revelation, a revelation underscored by the cocoon of transparent veils around the Child. If the panel is a predella, as seems likely, it would have been seen across an altar table, and these veils would have found their analogue in the altar-cloths, notably the fine white cloth known as the corporal, which was used to cover the paten and chalice. Filippino was surely well aware of the interplay between his pictorial veils and altar-cloths and textile furnishings. For his altar-piece for the Otto di Pratica in the Palazzo della Signoria he was paid to supply a blue curtain.[36]

Technically accomplished though he is, Filippino was tied to the symbolic modes he inherited from his father. He never quite adjusted to how Leonardo had changed the rules of the game by re-envisaging the function of chiaroscuro and the subtle blending of transitions known as *sfumato*. As Alexander Nagel has perceptively described it, Leonardo's *sfumato* internalised within painting itself the traditional alternation between veiling and revealing the sacred image, making it 'the prerogative of painting'.[37] This new manner of painting in *sfumato* asserted the 'autonomous status of painting', freeing it – one might say – from the stifling paraphernalia of actual curtains and vestments, and instead realising a mode of unveiling proper to itself.

Raphael was the painter who most inventively took up this new reflexive mode in which painting enacts its own unveiling. *The Bridgewater Madonna* in Edinburgh (fig.11), the *Madonna of the Diadem* in the Louvre, and the much-replicated *Madonna di Loreto* (fig.12) all exemplify this.[38] Something all three have in common is playfulness. And here I am going to risk another foray into psycho-analytic literature. According to writers on 'object relations', the growth of an infant's sense of distinction between its body and the world is marked by an inter-mediate stage in which familiar objects are intimately known through touch as much as sight. D.W. Winnicott called these 'transitional objects' because the infant does not fully differentiate them from their bodies, yet they extend the zone of bodily experience, creating the child's first links with the world 'out there'. A blanket is the most typical of these 'me-not-me' transitional objects.[39] When a blanket, towel, sheet or napkin is used in the game of bo-peep or peep-bo, the alternation of hiding and revealing the infant behind the veil affirms its growing sense of self. Of course the game can only be played with the cooperation and complicity of an older person who pretends the infant has disappeared and is overjoyed to see the same infant revealed again. The transitional object, initially known through touch, is now drawn into the reciprocal activity of seeing and being seen. In the images

FIG.11 | RAPHAEL (1483–1520)
The Virgin and Child ('The Bridgewater Madonna'), c.1507
Oil and gold on canvas, transferred from panel 81 × 55cm
National Gallery of Scotland, Edinburgh (Bridgewater Loan, 1945)

FIG.12 | RAPHAEL (1483–1520)
Madonna di Loreto, 1509–10
Oil on wood 120 × 90cm
Musée Condé, Chantilly

we are considering, veils are drawn into comparable play between touching and seeing, and they establish complicity in the eyes of the viewer. The Christ Child's transitional object – its link with 'the world out there' – becomes, in the pictorial veil, the sign of his future destiny.

Winnicott, discussing this crucial role of play between parent and infant, points out that this 'play is in fact neither a matter of inner psychic reality nor a matter of external reality', rather it exists in a potential space between the child and its environment.[40] By analogy – and it is only an analogy – I would suggest we cannot read the relation between Mother and Child in *The Bridgewater Madonna* in terms of any literal or physical space but rather as a potential space, which is also in this case the space of dream.[41] The Child grasps at a sash-like golden veil. Chromatically it is linked to the girdle knotted at her breast. With the finger and thumb of her right hand she touches, but does not restrain, her Child, while with the fingers and thumb of her left hand she touches her girdle. Mother and Child, Bride and Groom, both touch the golden strands of the veil-girdle. Its detachment suggests it is not quite integral to her dress (unlike the white veil around her neckline), rather it belongs to imaginative space – or one might say, prophetic space.

Hans Belting has argued that the religious art of the Middle Ages essentially belongs to the era of the image, before the advent of the era of art.[42] In the icon, at least in its paradigmatic form, there is a magical identity of what is depicted and the object as bearer of depiction. With the advance of the era of artistic self-consciousness this magical identity was undermined. Now appearance had to be staged. A reflexive process set in, whereby the artwork signalled its own revelation. In the *Madonna di Loreto* the transparent veil raised over the naked Child is at once a figure of revelation and a sign of Christ's flesh as sacrificial offering.[43] Raphael stages Paul's theology of Christ's flesh as the veil in terms of play between Mother and Child. The beholder of Raphael's Madonna does not simply see the sacred image, but witnesses the unveiling of the body of Christ.

Raphael was the master of bringing religious and artistic epiphany into mutual alliance, and *The Sistine Madonna* (fig.13) has long been recognised as a supreme example of this.[44] But the *Donna Velata* (fig.14), who is both sheathed and disclosed within her Juno-esque veil, is no less about the staging of appearance.[45]

FIG.13 | RAPHAEL (1483–1520)
The Sistine Madonna, 1512/13
Oil on canvas 269.5 × 201cm
Gemäldegalerie Alte Meister, Staatliche Kunstsammlungen Dresden

FIG.14 │ RAPHAEL (1483–1520)
The Veiled Woman, or La Donna Velata, c.1516
Oil on canvas 85.1 × 64.1cm
Palazzo Pitti, Florence

FIG.15 │ TITIAN (*c.*1485/90–1576)
The Annunciation, 1562–4
Oil on canvas 403 × 235cm
Church of San Salvatore, Venice

FIG.16 | TITIAN (WORKSHOP)
Toilet of Venus, late 16th century
Oil on canvas 94.3 × 73.8cm
The Samuel Courtauld Trust, The Courtauld Gallery, London

FIG.17 | TITIAN (c.1485/90–1576)
Venus with a Mirror, c.1555
Oil on canvas 124.5 × 105.5cm
Andrew W. Mellon Collection
National Gallery of Art, Washington DC

By the time of Raphael any ambitious artist was familiar with the story recorded by Pliny in his *Natural History* of the contest between Xeuxis and Parrhasius, in which Parrhasius triumphed by painting a curtain over his picture, which so deceived Xeuxis that he stepped forward to remove it.[46] Increasingly curtains and veils shifted from their primary association with veiling the sacred to manifesting artistry, but what is intriguing is that veils, however re-contextualised, retained some of their religious aura. When, in 1493, Eleanora of Aragon saw the wardrobe of her daughter Beatrice d'Este, she exclaimed that it was so well stocked with fine fabrics it reminded her of a church sacristy with priests' vestments and altar frontals.[47] Half a century later, Pietro Aretino, the friend of Titian, and tireless writer of religious tracts and erotic texts, remarked of a portrait of a beautiful lady, '*una donna bella*', that it was kept covered with fine silk as if it was a sacred relic – '*a guisa di reliquia*'.[48] By 1621 Raphael's *Donna Velata*, which was then in the Guardaroba Medicea, Florence, was recorded as covered with a curtain of red silk.[49]

Of all painters it was Titian who drew most creatively on parallels between sacred and mythological veils and curtains. Perhaps the most potent connection between these spheres is to be found in the figure of the bride. I have alluded already to the Virgin Mary as the Bride of Christ. In Titian's *Annunciation* (fig.15), a painting still above its altar in the Venetian church of San Salvatore, she lifts her veil from her face with a gesture that can be traced back to the goddess Juno (or Hera) lifting her veil before her husband Jupiter.[50] Titian deployed an almost identical gesture of lifting the veil in his painting of the *Toilet of Venus*. The original version of this appears to be lost, but it is known from many copies, workshop replicas and variants, including one in the Courtauld Gallery collection (fig.16). Within the theatre of Titian's studio, where paintings were kept on the go for many years, Venus and the Madonna could well exchange their veils.

The *Toilet of Venus* thematises two modes of seeing and showing. The diaphanous veil lifted from her face presents seeing through – sign of perspicuity and openness to the lover's gaze – whereas the mirror held up by cupid presents a reflexive act of seeing in. Another painting, *Venus with a Mirror* belonging to the National Gallery of Art in Washington (fig.17), and recently the poster girl for the exhibition *Titian, Tintoretto, Veronese* in the Louvre, is somewhat different. It was painted around 1555.[51] At this date, paintings of an erotic nature – such as that of Aretino's '*bella donna*' – were often kept covered by a curtain, and only revealed to suitable visitors. The curtain drawn back to the left, in the Washington canvas, may well have been seen by sixteenth-century viewers in relation to the real curtain that may have hung close to the surface of the painting. Marcantonio Michiel, in his accounts of visits to private palaces in Venice and the Veneto, which he wrote in the first decades of the sixteenth century, took pains to record the presence of mirrors as well as paintings, almost as though steel mirrors – or even better the latest invention, a mirror of *cristallo* glass from Murano – were equivalent to painted portraits.[52] It is also known that at this time mirrors were covered by drapes on special occasions, such as periods of mourning. Few observers have noticed that in the Washington picture the cupid on the right, who holds up the mirror, has also just unveiled it. The paint around his left hand is damaged but a dark blue drape is evidently bunched beneath his hand and hangs below the mirror. Because of the damage, it is difficult to interpret this gesture, but once we register this cloth, and how it could be lifted up to conceal the mirrored Venus, we recognise a secret symmetry with Venus's own gesture as she – in an echo of the modest gesture of a Venus *pudica* – gathers up her fur-trimmed velvet jacket around her waist.

So Titian's Venus offers the viewer a game of hide-and-seek, of veiling and unveiling. The substance of the paint, especially where it describes drapes and fabrics, establishes richly palpable surfaces; yet the mirrored image is fractured and elusive. Embodiment within the facture of Titian's paint is accompanied by a movement of withholding. This mode of veiling – this delaying of total apprehension – no longer takes the form of *sfumato* or blending of delicate glazes of translucent paint so much as a deliberate roughening of the grain. Viewed close up the brush-strokes make no sense; only from a distance do they cohere.

The Washington *Venus* was painted around 1555, the San Salvatore *Annunciation* around 1560, and it was between these dates that Titian painted his *poesie* (poetic narratives) of *Diana and Actaeon* (fig.18) and *Diana and Callisto* (fig.19). Essentially they turn the theme of unveiling into a tragic mode, albeit with comic undertones.[53] As I have written about these pictures elsewhere, I shall be brief.[54] Ovid

FIG.18 | TITIAN (c.1485/90–1576)
Diana and Actaeon, 1556–9
Oil on canvas 184.5 × 202.2cm
Purchased jointly by the National Galleries of Scotland
and the National Gallery, London, with contributions
from The Scottish Government, the National Heritage
Memorial Fund, The Monument Trust, The Art Fund
(with a contribution from the Wolfson Foundation) and
through public appeal, 2009

FIG.19 | TITIAN (*c*.1485/90–1576)
Diana and Callisto, 1556–9
Oil on canvas 187 × 204.5cm
National Gallery of Scotland, Edinburgh (Bridgewater Loan, 1945)

in his account of how Actaeon stumbled upon Diana and her nymphs bathing makes no mention of a curtain. Titian has hung the red drape on the left of the painting to dramatise Actaeon's fateful viewing of the goddess. Examined closely this makeshift curtain appears to be a great regal cloak with a dagged or scalloped hem. Pictorially it is the counterpart to the white veil with which Diana hastily but ineffectually tries to conceal her nakedness. But as in the Washington Venus, the cloths that might block and interrupt our vision are counterposed to reflecting surfaces in the form of the small mirror beneath the arm of the nymph on the left and the glassy surface of the water extending below. The carafe of clear *cristallo* glass may function as a symbol of the perspicuous – of the fateful openness of the view to Actaeon's gaze.

The theme of discovering, uncovering, laying open to sight, is no less central to *Diana and Callisto*. Here, as in the San Salvatore *Annunciation*, Titian's imagination takes off from a grand narrative of drapes and unfolds in every detail of his composition down to the smallest fluttering cloth. Diana sits regally beneath an improvised canopy, and opposite her the fall of its folds is answered by the lifting of Callisto's smock to reveal her pregnancy. Titian tosses up – quite arbitrarily – a gauzy veil to flutter above the shoulders of the nymph behind Callisto, and this insubstantial fabric is played against the obdurate hardness of the plinth behind her, where, roughly sketched in the relief, another veil billows behind a running huntress. On this great canvas, as in its companion piece *Diana and Actaeon*, the veils and curtains, that in the cult images of the Middle Ages signalled sacred presence, are now caught up in an art of discovering.

BIBLIOGRAPHY

ALBERTI 1972
Leon Battista Alberti, *On Painting; and, On Sculpture: the Latin texts of 'De pictura' and 'De statua' by Leon Battista Alberti*, Cecil Grayson (ed. and trans.), London, 1972

ALPERS 2005
Svetlana Alpers, *The Vexations of Art: Velázquez and Others*, New Haven and London, 2005

ARETINO 1957–60
Pietro Aretino, *Lettere sull'arte di Pietro Aretino*, Ettore Camesasca (ed.), 3 vols., Milan, 1957–60

BECKETT 2009
Samuel Beckett, *The Letters of Samuel Beckett 1929–1940*, Martha Dow Fehsenfeld and Lois More Overbeck (eds.), Cambridge, 2009

BELTING 1994
Hans Belting, *Likeness and Presence: A History of the Image before the Era of Art*, Edmund Jephcott (trans.), Chicago, 1994

BIANCHINI 1722
Giuseppe Maria Bianchini, *Notizie istoriche intorno all sacratissima Cintola di Maria Vergine che si conserva nella città di Prato in Toscana*, Florence, 1722

BON VALSASSINA AND GARIBALDI 1994
Caterina Bon Valsassina and Vittoria Garibaldi, *Dipinti, sculture e ceramiche della Galleria Nazionale dell'Umbria: Studi e restauri*, Florence, 1994

BRIGSTOCKE 1978
Hugh Brigstocke, *Italian and Spanish Paintings in the National Gallery of Scotland*, Edinburgh, 1978

BYNUM 1986
Caroline Walker Bynum, 'The Body of Christ in the Later Middle Ages: A Reply to Leo Steinberg', *Renaissance Quarterly*, vol.39, 1986, pp.399–439

CADOGAN 2009
Jean K. Cadogan, 'The Chapel of the Holy Belt in Prato: Piety and Politics in Fourteenth-Century Tuscany', *artibus et historiae*, no.60, 2009, pp.107–38

CARTWRIGHT 1905
Julia Cartwright, *Beatrice d'Este, Duchess of Milan (1475–1497): A Study of the Renaissance*, London, 1905

CASSIDY 1991
Brendan Cassidy, 'A Relic, Some Pictures and the Mothers of Florence in the Late Fourteenth Century', *Gesta*, vol.30, no.2, 1991, pp.91–9

CASSIDY 1992
Brendan Cassidy, 'Orcagna's Tabernacle in Florence: Design and Function', *Zeitschrift für Kunstgeschichte*, 55, 1992, pp.180–211

DRURY 1999
John Drury, *Painting the Word: Christian Pictures and their Meanings*, New Haven and London, 1999

EDINBURGH 2004
Peter Humfrey et al., *The Age of Titian: Venetian Renaissance Art from Scottish Collections*, National Gallery of Scotland, Edinburgh, 2004

EISENBERG 1989
Marvin Eisenberg, *Lorenzo Monaco*, Princeton, N.J., 1989

ELAM 2007
Caroline Elam, *Roger Fry's Journey: From the Primitives to the Post-Impressionists*, (The Watson Gordon Lecture 2006), Edinburgh, 2007

EVANGELATOU 2003
Maria Evangelatou, 'The Purple Thread of the Flesh: The Theological Connotations of a Narrative Iconographic Element in Byzantine Images of the Annunciation', in *Icon and Word: The Power of Images in Byzantium: Studies Presented to Robin Cormack*, Antony Eastmond and Liz James (eds.), Aldershot, 2003, pp.261–79

FERRARA 2007
Mauro Natale, *Cosme Tura e Francesco del Cossa: L'arte a Ferrara nell'età di Borso d'Este*, Palazzo dei Diamanti and Palazzo Schifanoia, Ferrara, 2007

HAMBURGER 2004
Jeffrey Hamburger, 'Body vs. Book: The Trope of Visibility in Images of Christian-Jewish polemic', in *Ästhetik des Unsichtbaren*, David Ganz and Thomas Lentes (eds.), Berlin, 2004, pp.112–45

HAMBURGER 2006
Jeffrey Hamburger, 'The Medieval Work of Art: Wherein the "Work"? Wherein the "Art"?', in *The Mind's Eye: Art and Theological Argument in the Middle Ages*, Jeffrey Hamburger and Anne-Marie Bouché (eds.), Princeton, N.J., 2006, pp.374–414

HILLS 1999
Paul Hills, *Venetian Colour: Marble, Mosaic, Painting and Glass*, New Haven and London, 1999

HILLS 2006
Paul Hills, 'Titian's Veils', *Art History*, vol.25, 2006, pp.771–95

HOOD 1993
William Hood, *Fra Angelico at San Marco*, New Haven and London, 1993

JONES AND PENNY 1983
Roger Jones and Nicholas Penny, *Raphael*, New Haven and London, 1983

KENNEDY 1938
Ruth Wedgwood Kennedy, *Alesso Baldovinetti: A Critical and Historical Study*, New Haven and London, 1938

KESSLER 2000
Herbert Kessler, *Spiritual Seeing: Picturing God's Invisibility in Medieval Art*, Philadelphia, 2000

KOUNENI 2008
Lenia Kouneni, 'The *Kykkotissa* Virgin and its Italian Appropriation', *artibus et historiae*, no.57, 2008, pp.95–107

KREYTENBERG 2000
Gert Kreytenberg, *Orcagna, Andrea di Cione: Ein universeller Künstler der Gotik in Florenz*, Mainz, 2000

KRISTEVA 1982
Julia Kristeva, *Powers of Horror: An Essay on Abjection*, Leon S. Roudiez (trans.), New York, 1982

LIGHTBOWN 2004
Ronald Lightbown, *Carlo Crivelli*, New Haven and London, 2004

LLEWELLYN-JONES 2003
Lloyd Llewellyn-Jones, *Aphrodite's Tortoise: The Veiled Woman of Ancient Greece*, Swansea, 2003

LONDON 1994
Jonathan Alexander (ed.), *The Painted Page: Italian Renaissance Book Illumination 1450–1550*, Royal Academy of Art, London; The Pierpont Morgan Library, New York, 1994

LONDON 2001
Beverly Brown (ed.), *The Genius of Rome 1592–1623*, Royal Academy of Arts, London; Palazzo Venezia, Rome, 2001

MANCINI 1956
Giulio Mancini, *Considerazioni sulla pittura / Viaggio per Roma*, Adriana Marucci and Luigi Salerno, (eds.), vol.1, Rome, 1956

MEYER ZUR CAPELLEN 2001–8
Jürg Meyer zur Capellen, *Raphael: A Critical Catalogue of his Paintings*, 3 vols., Landshut, 2001–8

MILANESI 1906
Gaetano Milanesi, *Le opere di Giorgio Vasari*, vol.III, Florence, 1906

MUSACCHIO 1999
Jacqueline Musacchio, *The Art and Ritual of Childbirth in Renaissance Italy*, New Haven and London, 1999

NAGEL 1993
Alexander Nagel, 'Leonardo and *sfumato*', *Res: Anthropology and Aesthetics*, no.24, Autumn 1993, pp.7–20

NEFF 1998
Amy Neff, 'The pain of *Compassio*: Mary's Labor at the Foot of the Cross', *Art Bulletin*, vol.80, 1998, pp.254–73

NEW YORK 2008
Andrea Bayer (ed.), *Art and Love in Renaissance Italy*, New York, 2008

PARDO 1997
Mary Pardo, 'Veiling the *Venus of Urbino*', in *Titian's Venus of Urbino*, Rona Goffen (ed.), Cambridge, 1997, pp.108–28

PARIS 2009
Vincent Delieuvin and Jean Habert (eds.), *Titien, Tintoret, Véronèse: rivalités à Venise*, Musée du Louvre, Paris, 2009

PFEIFFER 1987
Heinrich Pfeiffer, 'Raffael und die Theologie', in *Raffael in Seiner Zeit*, Volker Hoffmann (ed.), Nuremberg, 1987, pp.99–117

ROME 2008
Mauro Lucco and Giovanni Carlo Federico Villa (eds.), *Giovanni Bellini*, Scuderie del Quirinale, Rome, 2008

SCHMIDT 2007
Victor M. Schmidt, 'Curtains, *Revelatio*, and Pictorial Reality in Late Medieval and Renaissance Italy', in *Weaving, Veiling, and Dressing: Textiles and their Metaphors in the Late Middle Ages*, Kathryn M. Rudy and Barbara Baert (eds.), Turnhout, 2007, pp.191–214

SIENA 2003
Alessandro Bagnoli et al., *Duccio: Alle origini della pittura senese*, Santa Maria della Scala, Museo dell'Opera del Duomo, Siena, 2003

THOROLD 1896
Algar Thorold (trans.), *The Dialogue of the Seraphic Virgin, Catherine of Siena: dictated by her, while in a state of ecstasy, to her secretaries, and completed in the year of our Lord 1370*, London, 1896

WINNICOTT 2005
D.W. Winnicott, *Playing and Reality*, with a new preface by F. Robert Rodman, London and New York, 2005

ZAMBRANO AND NELSON 2004
Patrizia Zambrano and Jonathan Katz Nelson, *Filippino Lippi*, Milan, 2004

NOTES & REFERENCES

1. Giulio Mancini, writing around 1620, argued that sexually provocative images were most appropriate for bedrooms where they could be kept covered and only unveiled by the owner to his consort or a confidante who would not be shocked: Mancini 1956, p.143; see Beverly Brown's comment in her essay 'Between the Sacred and Profane', in London 2001, p.286.

2. See Belting 1994, especially the last chapter.

3. For the earlier Madonnas see Kreytenberg 2000, pp.100–2. Kreytenberg, p.108, discusses the architectural form as symbol of her virginity and the cupola as 'Abbild des Kosmos', as well as the association with domed Marian churches, and notably the Pantheon as symbol of the Mother of God. See also Cassidy 1992; for the statutes see p.182, with the original document cited in n.33; Cassidy also comments on the relation between sculpted curtains and the shutters and veils, pp.189–90.

4. Noted by Kreytenberg. Cassidy 1992, pp.190–4, argues that the space within the arcades was not originally intended to accommodate an altar but rather was a space for about four to six singers and musicians to perform the Lauds. Music-making angels are carved in the stone surround of the Madonna.

5. Brigstocke 1978, no.1904, pp.36–8, notes that 'the frame has been extensively restored'.

6. Kouneni 2008, for the origins of the type.

7. Exodus 26:31–3.

8. Mark 15:38.

9. Paul expounds his theology of Christ as high priest, veil and sacrifice at length in Hebrews chapters 6–10; for Christ's flesh as the veil, Hebrews 10:19–20. I treat this at slightly greater length in Hills 2006, pp.773–4. For the veil being done away see II Corinthians 3:12–18. Herbert Kessler discusses the veil of the temple in Christian exegesis in several essays which are collected in Kessler 2000; see especially chapter 3, 'Medieval Art as Argument', pp.53–63, and chapter 5, 'Gazing at the Future: The *Parousia* miniature in Vatican Cod. gr. 699', pp.88–103. For an analogy between the opening of the wound in Christ's side by the lance and rending of the veil of the temple, see Hamburger 2004, p.117.

10. See Siena 2003, cat.30, pp.198–9, entry by Victor M. Schmidt, which gives references to texts describing how at the Crucifixion the Madonna gave her veil to be Christ's loincloth. In his introductory essay in the same exhibition cata-logue Luciano Bellosi comments on Duccio's introduction of transparent veils, pp.133–5. The Perugia Madonna is close in spirit to the triptych by Duccio in the National Gallery in London. The significance of veiling and seeing in the London triptych is nowhere described better than in Drury 1990, pp.32–7.

11. For 'the thread of the flesh' that linked the Virgin and Christ at the Annunciation see the commentary in Evangelatou 2003, especially pp.263–5.

12. Hamburger 2006, p.402 – alluding to Hebrews chapter 10.

13. Amongst many discussions of the protective mantle see Belting 1994, pp.354–8.

14. Brigstocke 1978, pp.71–2; Eisenberg 1989, p.95. Both these authors date the painting about 1418 and point to workshop assistance in the execution.

15. Baldovinetti treated swaddling in a slightly earlier, much damaged, Madonna in the Mackay Collection: see Kennedy 1938, fig.87, and pp.92–7; for the Louvre Madonna see *ibid.* pp.120–9 for a fine description of its formal patterns but only a passing reference (p.123) to the swaddling. It is interesting to note that Baldovinetti's Madonna was admired by Samuel Beckett in 1938; see Beckett 2009, p.214.

16. Elam 2007, pp.20–4.

17. Cassidy 1991. Cassidy refers to the story of a noble Florentine matron who wove a thread from a single tassel of the girdle into a veil; when the veil was laid over a woman in labour who could not give birth, she gave birth free of danger (p.97). See also Cadogan 2009. For the legends surrounding the *Sacra cintola* see Bianchini 1722.

18. For examples see New York 2008.

19. Musacchio 1999, p.142.

20. See Lightbown 2004, plate 40; his text on pp.143–53, gives an exhaustive account of the altarpiece, with close observation of Crivelli's textiles.

21. Lightbown 2004, pp.209–16.

22. Brigstocke 1978, pp.44–5; Brown 2003; Ferrara 2007, cat.no.149, p.464.

23. Piero's works painted for the d'Este in Ferrara are lost. Another argument for an earlier dating of the Edinburgh Madonna is the affinity of the landscape featuring conical hills with those of Jacopo Bellini (*c.*1400–1470/71), such as that of the *Virgin and Child with a Member of the d'Este Family*, in the Louvre (see Hills 1999, fig.115).

24. The altarpiece from San Domenico in Ascoli is dated 1476.

25. The membrane appears more like parchment than cloth. Occasionally at this date paintings were executed on vellum laid onto panel, for example *Christ's Descent into Limbo*, attributed to Giovanni Bellini, in the City Museum and Art Gallery, Bristol.

26. In an era before the definition of landscape painting as a category, such intangible distances will be referred to as '*lontani*' in a letter from Michele Viannello to Isabella d'Este about a Nativity ('*Prexepio*') by Giovanni Bellini, dated November 3rd 1502: Rome 2008, document 77, p.348.

27. See the entry by Lilian Armstrong in London 1994, cat.no.96, pp.190–2.

28. Alberti 1972, p.55: *De pictura*, Bk.I, para.19.

29. Examples may be seen very clearly in a couple of the scenes of *Miracles of San Bernardino of Siena*, dated 1473, in the National Gallery of Umbria in Perugia: Bon Valsassina and Garibaldi 1994, cat. no.47, b and f, pp.209–21 (with colour plates).

30. Alberti 1972, pp.68–9: *De pictura*, Bk.II, para.31. I thank Roger Tarr for reminding me of this veil. For an ingenious discussion of Alberti's veil and other textile analogies see Pardo 1997.

31. Thorold 1896, chapters XXI–XXXI; the text is discussed in Hood 1993, p.110.

32. Kristeva 1982.

33. Neff 1998. I thank John Lowden for this reference.

34. Bynum 1986, p.424.

35. Brigstocke 1978, pp.68–9. For the *Dead Christ with Two Angels*, see Zambrano and Nelson 2004, cat.58, p.601.

36. Filippino was paid for expenses relating to 'la tenda azzurra, per la frangia di seta bianca e rossa

e per alcune lavori di legname': Milanesi 1906, p.474, n.2. For curtains in front of paintings, and further bibliography, see Schmidt 2007.

37. Nagel 1993.

38. For a recent catalogue with references to earlier bibliography see Meyer zur Capellen 2001–8: *Bridgewater Madonna*, vol.1, cat.33, pp.250–3; *Madonna of the Diadem*, vol.2, cat.A9, pp.251–4; *Madonna di Loreto*, vol.2, cat.51, pp.89–97.

39. Winnicott's 'Transitional Objects and Transitional Phenomena' is the first essay in his collection *Playing and Reality*, first published in 1971 and now available in Winnicott 2005, pp.1–34. 'Me-not-me' is a characterisation of Alpers 2005, p.29.

40. From the essay, 'The Location of Cultural Experience', reprinted in Winnicott 2005, pp.128–39, quotation from p.129.

41. c.f. Jones and Penny 1983, p.36: 'The child appears to have woken, having perhaps dreamt of the Passion'.

42. Belting 1994.

43. Pfeiffer 1987, pp.101–3, offers a marginally different theological interpretation of the painting, connecting the veil both to the veil of the Veronica and to the *Thalamus*, or bridal chamber of Christ and the Virgin: '...*das Liegen des Jesuskindes auf dem grossen Brautbett, dem Thalamus*'. However, the presence of Joseph seems like an intrusion if the bridal chamber is of major significance. The darkened background of the painting at Chantilly represented a green curtain: if the raised veil alludes to the veil of the Holy of Holies, the curtain may allude to the outer curtains of the tabernacle.

44. Meyer zur Capellen 2001–8, vol.II, cat.53, pp.107–16; pp.112–14 offer a fair summary of the extensive literature on the curtain in Raphael's altarpiece.

45. Meyer zur Capellen 2001–8, vol.III, cat.73, pp.116–19.

46. Book XXXIV, 65.

47. Cartwright 1905, p.171.

48. Aretino 1957–60, vol.I, letter CLIII, p.225.

49. Meyer zur Capellen 2001–8, vol.III, p.119, note 67, '...*con sua cortina di ermisino rosso guarnita di frangia di seta rossa e cordone di seta simile*'.

50. I have discussed the veils in this altarpiece in Hills 2006, pp.783–5. For the gesture of raising the veil, known as *anaklypsis*, see Llewellyn-Jones 2003, pp.84–120: I thank Peter Stewart for this reference.

51. Paris 2009, cat.29, p.228.

52. I discuss this in Hills 1999, p.186.

53. In the lecture I only mentioned the 'tragic mode': afterwards Elizabeth Cowling shrewdly remarked upon the comic element in *Diana and Actaeon*.

54. Hills 2006, pp.786–90. For a recent account of the paintings see Peter Humfrey's entries in Edinburgh 2004, cats.54–5, pp.157–62.